BE YOURSELF

AND OTHER BAD ADVICE

BE YOUR

AND OTHER BAD ADVICE

SELF

A Teen Girl's Guide to Unlearning the Rules

MEREDITH WALKER

ILLUSTRATED BY NINA COSFORD

Workman Kids • New York

Workman Kids
Workman Publishing
Hachette Book Group, Inc.
1290 Avenue of the Americas
New York, NY 10104
workman.com

Workman Kids is an imprint of Workman Publishing, a division of Hachette Book Group, Inc. The Workman name and logo are registered trademarks of Hachette Book Group, Inc.

Design by Sara Corbett

Library of Congress Cataloging-in-Publication Data is on file.

ISBNs: 978-1-5235-2503-4 (trade paperback); 978-1-5235-3718-1 (ebook); 978-1-6686-5802-4 (audio)

First Edition March 2026

Printed in Guangdong, China (01/26) 1010 on responsibly sourced paper

10 9 8 7 6 5 4 3 2 1

*For anyone trying to
figure out who they are,
what they think, and
what being yourself
even means,
this is for you.*

—M. W.

CONTENTS

Foreword

BY AMY POEHLER

Welcome, Reader!

Are you looking to AVOID FAILURE?
Do you want to FIGURE EVERYTHING OUT?
Feeling ready to finally BE PERFECT?

Well, I have some bad news for you. That is impossible.

But here is some good news. This book is still for you.

Let me first start by saying congratulations on reading a book! It's not easy these days to focus while the robots distract you with pictures of a hairbrush that plays music. Secondly, congratulations on deciding to be curious about yourself. Getting to know who you are is a lifelong process. It never stops and is always full of surprises, which is why this book has found you at the perfect time.

In 2001, Meredith Walker and I met at *Saturday Night Live* and became instant friends. Almost twenty-five years later, we remain chosen sisters who care deeply about each other and the world. In 2008, we created an online community called Smart Girls that came out of a simple desire to hear young women tell us their stories. We were curious about how people saw their own lives and the choices they made. *What makes you a good sister? Why do you like to box? Do you agree that animals are better than most humans?* We got to laugh and cry and dance together, all the while remembering that we need to be gentle with ourselves as we trudge through this one wild and precious life.

In *Be Yourself and Other Bad Advice*, Meredith continues to be curious, but she asks us to join in. She asks us to start the most important conversation we will have in our whole life. A conversation that never stops and never gets old. A conversation that we should have all the time and only needs one person around to happen. A conversation with ourselves. So, reader . . . what do we care about? What have we failed at? Are we ready to get out of our comfort zone?

Imagine how much you know about soccer or superheroes or Lady Gaga. Now imagine doing that same research on yourself. What if you examined yourself as closely as you do a fossil? What if you held yourself gently while you turned your life over and over in your hand? Treat this book like a new pair of glasses that can help you finally see the wonderful things in front of you. There is only one YOU, and that YOU is a mystery filled with delicious clues. This book can point you in the right direction so you can find who did it! (News flash: IT WAS YOU!)

So good luck on your journey. We are taking the ride right along with you. And we can't wait to hear what you find out.

Introduction

My first day at *Saturday Night Live* felt exactly like being the new kid at school: pretending I was calmer than I was, wondering who my friends would be, and trying to find out where the bathrooms were.

I knew I'd eventually figure it out, but I also knew it would be awkward for a while.

On that first day, another newbie and I were led around to meet everyone. The only weird thing was that our guide introduced us by name, but didn't mention our jobs or why we were there. My new friend and I kept glancing at each other, like, "Should we explain that we aren't contest winners or someone's cousins visiting from out of town?"

Honestly, part of me did feel like I'd won a contest. I was about to start working on one of my favorite TV shows of all time, with the opportunity to be part of comedy history, surrounded by funny, like-minded people—many of whom would become my lifelong friends. Who wouldn't feel lucky? At the same time, I knew I'd earned this. Years of interviewing kids, artists, and experts for news stories had taught me how to make people comfortable and bring out their best. Now I was about to become the head of the talent department, where I would get to book and take care of the hosts and musical guests on the show.

I stood there with my new friend, knowing we'd have to find our way. And we both did pretty well. I tried to infuse calm and kindness wherever I could, and even got to deliver a line in an opening monologue. And my friend? Her name is Maya Rudolph, and she's a comedy legend.

We all have those moments—feeling a little lost or unsure of what comes next. And that brings me to you.

THIS BOOK IS ABOUT YOU

This is really a book about you—a guide for finding out more about yourself, the person you are now,

and the person you are becoming. Along the way you will learn some practical ways to apply that knowledge to create a life that actually feels like yours.

We are already at a disadvantage here because social media moves faster than we can process our own thoughts. All the constant content implants ideas and images and expectations quicker than we can know what we think for ourselves. Social media platforms are where you are bombarded with "game changers," hacks, tips, hot takes, and glow-up advice telling you to "Be your best self!" Look better, eat better, hustle harder, and level up! Spend money, make money, then spend *more* money to look like everyone else does! But amid all that noise, there's one thing nobody's talking about enough: how to *think* for yourself.

Thinking for yourself comes from asking questions, staying curious, and trusting your judgment. It means being comfortable analyzing what's in front of you instead of just absorbing what someone else believes. Real confidence comes from forming your own opinions. As you go through these pages and follow the prompts, you might be listening to *my* opinions, but I hope you will be thinking for yourself more and more.

WHY SHOULD YOU TRUST ME?

Good question. I could list my professional résumé, but what really qualifies me to write this book is that I've been there, in the trenches of a messy young adult life. I spent years being a teenager, then stumbling through my twenties and thirties trying to find my way. I've been mean to people and had people be mean to me. I've wrestled with my insecurities. I've wondered what I was capable of and if I would ever make any progress. I've stood in rooms where I knew no one, wondering who my friends would be.

Here's what I've learned: Thinking for yourself allows you to truly know yourself. And knowing yourself—what drives you, what you care about, and what makes you *you*—is the foundation for building a life you love.

I started my career at *Nick News*, an award-winning show for young people on the cable channel Nickelodeon, designed to educate young viewers about historical and current events. We encouraged viewers to look at the world around them and ask important questions about what was happening and why. As part of that job, I traveled across the country, talking to kids, teens, and adults about their lives, their worries, and their hopes. Years later, at *Saturday Night Live*, I used those same skills to help nervous guest hosts feel cared about and supported before stepping onto live TV. Whether you're a kid sharing your story, an adult performing for millions of viewers, or a teenager figuring out your next steps, one thing is true: it helps so much to know someone cares about what you're going through.

And then there's Smart Girls, an online community I cofounded with my best friend, Amy Poehler. We clicked immediately when we met at *SNL*—she's super smart, good-hearted, and knows how to stick up for herself. We spent a lot of time hanging out, talking, playing Rummikub, and watching *Law & Order* reruns. Together, we created Smart Girls to encourage girls to live interesting lives—on their terms, not someone else's timeline or expectations.

For years, I've done something that has shaped the way I see the world: I've listened to young people. My work with Smart Girls has taken me from villages in Malawi and Syrian refugee camps in Jordan to rural clinics in Haiti, and high schools across the US. No matter where I go, I love hearing from girls about their challenges, their questions, and their hopes.

If you're anything like the teen girls I've met,

you might feel like every decision right now will make or break your future, like you're supposed to have it all figured out by age fourteen or eighteen or twenty-two or whatever. That's just not true. You don't need to have all the answers. You just need to start asking the right questions.

A GUIDE TO KNOWING WHAT YOU REALLY THINK

Whenever you sit down with this book, I hope you'll use it as a chance to check in with yourself. Maybe you'll think about something big, like the kind of future you want to shape for yourself. Maybe you'll unearth some opinions you hold, like beards without mustaches are weird.

The point is to discover and feel more connected with your own thoughts and beliefs. Are you following your own path? Are you making choices that feel right to you? What do you value? What makes you feel like yourself?

Knowing yourself is the best way to avoid handing your decisions over to someone else. It might feel easier to go along with what others want for you, but that can lead to you feeling disconnected from yourself, like you're just following expectations

without checking in with what you feel, think, or want. That can show up as second-guessing yourself a lot or feeling unsure about what you believe. But figuring out who you are doesn't happen out of nowhere. It's something you discover step by step. That's why I wrote this book: to help you take those steps so you can feel more sure of yourself, more in control, and more YOU.

BY THE TIME YOU FINISH

This isn't a "read it once and forget it" kind of book. Think of it like a conversation—one you'll come back to as you grow, change, and discover new things about yourself. This book gets you to ask: Who do I want to be? What do I care about? What do I like? And if you've ever wondered, "What do I think and how do I even figure out what I think?" you're not alone. That's what this book is for.

My hope is that, when you reach the last page, you'll know yourself a little better. Maybe you'll even have a moment where you think, "Whoa, I didn't know that about me!" And you will know for sure that you are interesting and worth getting to know.

Because you are.

So, what do you say? Let's get started!

WHAT DO
i FEEL?
WHAT DO
i BELIEVE?
WHOSE
VOICES DO
i LISTEN TO?
WHAT DO
i CARE ABOUT
iN THE
WORLD?
HOW DO
i TREAT
PEOPLE?
WHAT ARE
MY VALUES?
WHAT MAKES
ME FEEL GOOD
ABOUT MYSELF?
WHAT DO
i WANT
TO TRY?

WHO AM i?

CHAPTER 1

"BE YOURSELF."

Okay, but How Do I Actually Do That?

IF someone asked who you are deep down, what would you say?

You could answer that you're a tiny explosion of humanity made of stardust, atoms, and neurons, and you would be correct. Seriously. That is not snark, that's science. All atoms come originally from the stars, including the ones that make up the body you're living in right now. This isn't just fascinating trivia—it's a reminder that you're part of something vast and extraordinary. The same cosmic forces that shaped galaxies, oceans, and forests also shaped you. When you think about yourself this way, any quirks and "flaws" you might have fall into their proper perspective. You're not a stand-alone ball of confusion—you're part of something universal.

And yet, despite this magic, people often feel like there is something wrong with them or they're not enough. Why? Because society loves sending mixed messages. Be yourself—but not too much. Be confident—but don't act "bossy." Be body positive—but buy *this* to look like *this*. Fit in—but also stand out. It's exhausting!

And what does "Be Yourself" even mean? Are you supposed to walk into a party and casually announce how often you need to use tweezers or that you're obsessed with historical cooking videos? ("Hi, I'm Meredith, and I can tell you how the Romans made bread.")

Well, being yourself does not mean that you have to know exactly who you are all the time. It means simply accepting who you are now and letting yourself grow into the person you are becoming—on your own terms. When you know yourself, you aren't swallowed up by anyone else's opinions and expectations. You can move through the world trusting your instincts and building a life that feels like it is authentically yours. Living that way releases the pressure to fit into someone else's idea of you. A shift happens and you feel it. You feel wonderfully yourself. You're simply being you.

Understanding and appreciating yourself starts with noticing those times in your life when you feel most comfortable, when you can actually feel that you aren't trying so hard. You are just there, as is. That is the real you peeking through. An easy time to spot this is when you're laughing with your best friend, doing an activity that captures all of your attention, or even just listening to music you really love. It's the version of you that feels free and unjudged.

Being yourself can feel both freeing and terrifying. It's fun to explore your style, humor, and interests. But what about the parts of you that might not be accepted by others—your culture, sexuality, religion, or gender? It might not always feel safe to share those parts. Protecting yourself matters, too. You don't have to explain yourself to people who won't respect or understand you. What's important is that you grasp this: You deserve respect. Being yourself is for you—to understand and appreciate who you are even if others don't see it yet.

THE PRESSURE TO CONFORM

Being yourself can feel easier said than done. Girls are conditioned to change themselves for approval. Entire industries—beauty, wellness, supplements—are built on making us feel like we're not enough so they can sell us something. And it's not just ads or social media; sometimes, it's louder, bigger voices in positions of power.

There are still people in leadership positions who evaluate women not for their intelligence or character but for their physical attributes. Some men reduce women to numbers, rating them on a scale from one to ten or even referring to them as "pigs" or "dogs"—or worse. The way leaders talk about women can influence societal attitudes about them. Hearing degrading messages can get into girls' heads. If parents or friends support someone saying horrible things about women, it is no surprise that the daughters internalize these attitudes and start to believe their worth is tied to their appearance. But your worth isn't something others get to decide. It's already yours.

You'd think "being yourself" wouldn't still involve overcoming patriarchy, but here we are. Patriarchy—a way of organizing society where men have more power and control than women or over women—still exists. Some people celebrate it, dismiss gender equality, or treat women like we're less. Pay attention to the messages you hear. Do leaders show women respect? Do they try to control us through their words or policies? Are they making women feel included or excluded? These attitudes matter because they shape how we see ourselves. No matter what they say, you don't need outside approval to know you're valuable and complete. You are already whole. You don't need to prove your worth or wait for someone else to complete you.

FITTING IN vs. BEING REAL

When you're growing up, it can feel like your survival depends on fitting in. I remember times I went along with the crowd and acted mean just to belong. I've been the monster, and I've been the one hurt by other monsters. And being the monster never felt good—because pretending to be someone you're not always leaves you empty. It's like wearing a mask or disguise covering up the real you, and it's itchy and uncomfortable.

You are being yourself when your actions and words align with what you feel inside. Show up honestly—don't pretend to love the latest diss track if you'd rather listen to Brandi Carlile. Speak up when something feels wrong, like refusing to brush off a racist joke or a bigoted insult. If something feels bad or uncomfortable, listen to that feeling. Your instincts are smarter than you think. Trust them. Being true to yourself comes from listening to that inner voice and acting in a way that feels right, even when it's difficult.

Being yourself doesn't require you to lock into one identity forever. Change your mind, try new things. Trying on different identities—exploring styles, hobbies, and friend groups—is part of growing up. Maybe you're deep in your *folklore* phase, obsessed with vintage embroidery and poetry. Or you're experimenting with punk skater looks or a retro preppy aesthetic. That's all good. Just make sure you're genuinely into it and not faking it to impress someone else.

Fitting in by pretending will always feel hollow. Belonging—being seen and valued for your real self—feels pretty great.

DISCOVERING WHO YOU ARE

At Amy Poehler's Smart Girls, our motto was "Change the world by being yourself." It wasn't just an empty slogan; we meant it. Being yourself can be tough. It takes courage, but when you start to accept who you are—eccentricities, flaws, strengths, and all—life feels better. You feel better. And that makes the world better, at least because there's one less miserable person in it.

Take time to investigate what is way underneath the surface. Welcome the parts of you that are different, creative, or weird. Maybe this time next year, you'll be hosting a podcast about soap carving or playing lead cymbals in a drumline. Who knows? Follow what feels like you.

Being yourself is a verb. A process. A practice. You'll change, and that's a good thing. Some days you will feel confident and sure, and some days you will feel insecure and lost. Try not to worry about the fluctuations because you will be fine as long as you keep trying to be someone you can respect. No matter where you go, you'll always bring you with you—so make sure you like who that person is.

The most revolutionary act in a world that pressures you to conform is daring to be yourself. Right now, in this moment, you are worthy, wonderful, and complete. So go ahead, go off-script, try that weird idea, laugh as loud as you want to, and imagine big things for your life.

FIGURING OUT WHO YOU ARE

goes beyond surface-level details like your hair color or zip code. It takes recognizing the moments when you feel most relaxed, at ease, and proud. These moments point to your authentic self. Throughout this book, I'll offer some prompts to help you find those moments and dig down to what really matters.

Grab a journal or notebook and start things off with these questions below. Be honest—there are no wrong answers here.

Ready? Let's begin.

1 What Sparks Your Interests?

- Think about the last time you got lost in what you were doing. Where were you? What were you doing? Who were you with?
- What are you curious about? What topics or activities make you want to learn more?
- What feels fun to you? Not what *should* be fun, but what actually makes you feel like you are having fun?

- When do you feel most at ease, like you can fully relax and be yourself?
- What are you doing when you genuinely like yourself—when you're comfortable being exactly who you are?

Go back and review your answers. Do you notice any patterns? For example:

- Are you drawn to creativity, like art, music, or crafts?
- Do you feel most alive when you're helping others, solving problems, or learning something new?
- Are you energized by connection—making others laugh, sharing ideas, or building relationships?

These recurring themes are clues to what makes you feel fulfilled and grounded.

2 Describe Yourself.

Think of three adjectives to describe yourself that have nothing to do with your appearance.

- Examples: Considerate, adventurous, inquisitive, patient, determined, honest, funny

Think about the words you chose.

- Why did you choose these words? What do they reveal about you?
- How do these qualities show up in your daily life?
- What's one way you can dig into each quality this week? (For example, if "adventurous" is one of your words, what's a small adventure you could plan, like exploring a new place or trying something new?)

These adjectives point out some of your strengths. Try to find ways to apply them more and more into your daily life.

3 Find Your Proud Moments.

Think about times when you felt genuinely proud of yourself—not because someone else praised you, but because the things you did felt right to you. See if you can come up with at least three examples. These could be big or small:

- Drawing a sketch of the view out your window
- Cooking dinner for someone
- Helping a lost dog get home
- Making your sister laugh so hard she actually peed a little

Once you have your own list, think about this:

- What made these moments feel so good?
- Do your proud moments share anything in common?

Your proud moments reveal what genuinely matters to you. Look for patterns—they're clues to the activities and experiences that make you like yourself even more.

Keep exploring. Keep noticing. Keep being honest with yourself. When you live in alignment with who you truly are, you'll feel more confident and fulfilled—because you'll know you're showing up as you.

CHAPTER 2

What Is This Feeling, and What Can I Do About It?

Have you ever felt overwhelmed by your feelings? That crushing sense of sadness that happens when someone breaks up with you or you're in a big fight with a friend? Maybe you get a bad test score that makes you feel extreme self-disappointment. Or you find out you weren't invited to a party everyone else is going to—so you feel rejected and very lonely. Despite trying really hard to distract yourself, the heavy feelings persist, and you replay the situation repeatedly in your mind. You get stuck in a loop of crappy emotions that seem inescapable, and it feels BAD.

When emotions hit hard, it's easy to react without thinking, criticize yourself, or shove your feelings aside. But there is a different approach that is more helpful. Take a deep breath. Pause and ask yourself, "What is this feeling trying to tell me?" Give yourself a moment of curiosity. Most of the time, emotions are trying to get your attention for a reason.

EMOTIONS AS MESSAGES

Your emotions are like the light beam from a flashlight, illuminating what you need to pay attention to. Fear yells, "Danger! Get out of here!" while happiness whispers, "This feels right. Keep going." Sometimes, their messages are crystal clear, like the joy you feel while rehearsing for the school play with friends. Other times, like when you're heartbroken or rejected, emotions can feel unbearable—but they're still doing their job.

Experiencing deep sadness after a heartbreak means your emotions are working *properly*, even though it hurts. Yes, they are painful, but it's appropriate for your feelings to match the situation. The intensity of your feelings often reveals the significance of the things that resonate with you. Whatever the message, it's up to you to interpret and act on it.

Emotions are real, but they are not always 100% accurate. Especially the tough ones. They can exaggerate. They can mislead or overwhelm you, especially when they're negative. That's why learning about your emotions—and how to respond to them—is so much more helpful than sinking into them.

You have a choice: you can dwell on negative emotions and potentially make things worse, or you can become more aware of your feelings and practice responding appropriately. Responding appropriately means your reaction matches the scenario. Take it from me, a very emotionally intelligent person who (in her twenties) threw a raw egg at my brother because he made fun of my outfit.

WHY EMOTIONS FEEL SO INTENSE RIGHT NOW

If your emotions sometimes feel like they have the strength of a tornado, there's a scientific reason for that. Hormones kick everything up a notch, and puberty brings a surge of hormones that can make emotions more extreme. At the same time, your prefrontal cortex, the part of your brain that helps with decision-making and impulse control, is still growing, which means your emotions can spin out of control before your logical reasoning can catch up. Altogether, your brain is a construction zone that will continue to develop until you're about age twenty-five.

Girls in workshops I've led felt less overwhelmed after learning about this brain science. If you think about it, you're taught about physical changes to expect during adolescence—longer legs, acne, growing breasts. But brain development isn't visible; it's *experienced*, through intense, sometimes overwhelming emotions.

So, the next time you're in a horrible mood and acting like a brat, you can tell yourself, "I am not being dramatic! This is BIOLOGY!" Or just remind yourself that strong emotions are normal and manageable.

Your brain-growth years could be called your "Emotions Era"—a time when you are juggling big changes, strong feelings, and life experiences all at once. Adults may not always get this. They might say things like, "Why are you freaking out? It's just one party!" or the classic "Calm down." They don't always understand how something small to them can feel huge to you. That's why learning to settle yourself and manage your feelings is especially helpful. And a big part of that is practicing emotional awareness—the skill of noticing, naming, and accepting your emotions as they show up.

HOW TO HANDLE INTENSE FEELINGS

Did you know that strong emotions, like anger, sadness, or joy, usually peak within about ninety seconds? During that minute and a half, you might feel your heart race, your face flush, or your breathing change. After that, the intensity fades—if you let it.

Recognizing that this intensity is short-lived can be reassuring; it reminds you that even the most overwhelming feelings are temporary. So, when you're going through something tough, remember that this initial feeling will likely fizzle out and get easier to handle as time goes by.

When you do feel overwhelmed, the goal isn't to shove your feelings away but to handle them in healthy ways. You might think of it as a three-step process:

1

Express the emotion.

2

Name the emotion.

Choose your next actions.

In the first step, if you're feeling BIG FEELINGS, try to find a physical outlet to express them and help the emotion run its course. For example:

- Slam pillows around your room.
- Bang on drums.
- Go for a run or hike.
- Draw, write, or play music.
- Scream in the shower.
- Talk to someone you trust.

Whatever works for you, let it out in a way that won't hurt you or other people. Expressing emotions helps you process them and carry on.

Feel it all—without judging yourself for having those feelings. Whatever happened already hurt. Judging yourself for having the feelings only adds an extra layer of misery on top of whatever crappiness you're already going through. It isn't helpful, so let that self-judgment go and deal with your real feelings instead.

THE POWER OF YOUR THOUGHTS

The second step involves naming your feelings, which is really a matter of taking your *feelings* and turning them into *thoughts.* We do this because redirecting your thoughts has a powerful effect on redirecting your emotions. Let me show you what I mean. Try this: Close your eyes, take a deep breath, and imagine slicing a fresh lemon. Picture the bright yellow rind, feel its texture, and sense the give as the knife cuts through it. Now, imagine bringing a juicy slice to your mouth, taking a bite, and experiencing the sour taste. Notice your mouth watering or a tingling sensation.

The lemon isn't even real, but your brain sent signals to your body just from imagining it. That's the power of your thoughts—they influence your emotions and physical responses.

PRACTICE EMOTIONAL AWARENESS

Identifying your feelings is also known as "emotional awareness." Emotional awareness is the skill of acknowledging, naming, and accepting your emotions as they show up—no judgment, just observation. Let's try it right now: how do you feel? Maybe you'd say, "I feel content and inspired because this book is helping me learn more about myself." Congratulations, you just practiced emotional awareness!

Seriously, though, noticing and naming your feelings takes practice. But it doesn't have to be complicated. Start small. If you've seen *Inside Out*, then you know the main characters are

Joy, Fear, Sadness, Anger, and Disgust.

These are drawn from Dr. Paul Ekman's seven universal emotions and Dr. Robert Plutchik's eight primary emotions: joy, sadness, fear, anger, surprise, anticipation, trust, and disgust. (There are only five emotions in the film because they had to squeeze a lot into one movie.) Can you slot whatever you're feeling into one of those five to start?

Still, those emotions don't cover everything. Think about it. When someone asks how you are, how often do you just say "fine"? It's such a vague reply, it's more like a shrug than an answer. What if, instead, you said, "I'm feeling restless," or "I'm feeling hopeful," or "I'm feeling lonely" or "glum" or "eager" or "giddy"? Using precise words paints a clearer picture of what's going on inside you, and there are thousands of words you can use to describe how you feel. Start exploring them and see how much easier it becomes to understand yourself. (You can check out one of the explorations at the end of this chapter for some tools here.)

Try it! The next time you're watching a movie, hit pause when you feel a strong reaction and name the emotion.

Example: Watching *Titanic*, you see that Jack totally could have fit on that floating door with Rose. What do you feel? Rage? Sadness? Confusion? Can you identify exactly what is making you feel that way?

- **Go deeper:** "I feel rage because it's unfair, and Jack didn't have to die." Or "I feel a mix of sadness and confusion because he might have fit, but the door would have sunk under their combined weight."

Naming your emotions gives you a chance to consider what you're feeling, understand why you're feeling it, and respond in a smart way. The more you practice, the better you'll get.

WHERE DO YOU GO FROM HERE?

You've expressed your emotions. You've named your emotions. And now comes a crucial moment, the third step: What will you choose to do next?

Your emotions are your brain's way of sending you a message about your next course of action. Once you're calm enough to name your emotion, consider what that feeling is nudging you to do.

* FURIOUS?

That's your signal to speak up when something's not right. Say something, let others know about it, take action—whatever helps you stand up for what matters.

* **ANXIOUS?**

  That could mean "get ready." Create a plan, practice, study—do what you need to feel more in control.

* **GUILTY?**

  That's a signal to fix something. Own it, take accountability, apologize if needed, and repair by figuring out how to do better next time.

* **DISAPPOINTED?**

  That's a nudge to persevere. Make adjustments, try again, and remind yourself why this is important to you.

Then, whatever the feeling is, take a deep breath and do the thing you need to do.

Your emotions aren't out to get you—they're pointing you in the right direction. They're tools for understanding yourself, your values, and your life. Pay attention, then take the next step.

BUILDING YOUR EMOTIONAL VOCABULARY

Expanding your emotional vocabulary can help you understand yourself better and communicate your feelings more clearly. Here's how to start:

Search for "lists of emotions" online. Choose one link, look through the list, and see if any words resonate with feelings you've experienced but never knew how to name. Pay attention to the definitions, even for words you think you already know. Nuances in meaning can help you distinguish between similar emotions. For example, here are three different varieties of happiness:

- **Cheerful:** Positive and happy, but with a steady, upbeat quality that's deeper than a fleeting moment of joy.
- **Ecstatic:** Intensely happy or overjoyed, often from triumph. You're happy when your dad buys you a guitar, but you're ecstatic when the audience gives you a standing ovation for your guitar solo.

- **Delighted:** Pleased and satisfied—a calmer happiness, like a cozy contentment.

Now that you've looked at all those words, try to make them part of your everyday emotional vocabulary.

- Which new words stand out to you? Write them down.
- Think about the emotions you explored. When have you felt each one? Can you remember specific situations when you were "cheerful" or "ecstatic" rather than just "happy"?
- Consider this: How often do you default to vague words like "fine" or "okay" to describe your feelings? How might things change if you use more specific words?

This exercise is about more than just words. When you can name what you feel, you can better express it to others, and you'll also begin to see what kinds of experiences bring out the most meaningful emotions in you.

CHECKING IN WITH YOUR EMOTIONS

This activity will help you build awareness of your emotions in real time and notice how they shift throughout your day. Pick three moments to check in with yourself on one day. Choose times that are random but varied. For example:

- After a class
- While walking somewhere
- At the end of the day, when you're winding down

Each time, ask yourself the following questions:

- What am I feeling right now? (Use the six basic emotions from the text or the list you found above to source specific words.)
- Why am I feeling this way? What's happening around me? Who am I with? What am I thinking about?

- Are there certain places, people, or activities that tend to bring up positive or negative emotions for me?

Example Check-Ins:

- After a hard test "I feel relieved because I finished something that had been stressing me out."
- Walking home after dark "I feel anxious because the wind sounds eerie, and that guy over there has a beard but no mustache."
- Listening to music in my room "I feel content and calm because this music matches my mood."

If you can, jot down the time, circumstances, and feelings in your Notes app or a journal. Do this every day for a week, checking in with yourself three times each day. At the end of the week, assess:

- When did you feel the best? What were you doing?
- When did you feel the most drained or upset? Why?

- Were there any surprises? Did you discover an emotion you didn't expect?
- Look at your circumstances across the times you felt the worst or the best. Do you see any connections there? Any surprises?

This practice helps you notice patterns in your emotions. Over time, you'll learn what experiences energize you and bring joy, as well as what situations drain you or make you feel negative.

These exercises go beyond identifying emotions—they build a clearer picture of who you are and what makes you feel most alive. The more you practice, the better you'll understand yourself.

CHAPTER 3

Valuing Your Values Is Valuable

Questions like "Where do I belong?" "What do I stand for?" "What do I care about most?" are part of getting to know yourself. It's normal to look for clues everywhere: scrolling social media, watching shows, listening to your parents, following trends, or talking with friends. But when you're always soaking up everyone else's opinions and influences, it's hard to hear your own thoughts. That's why it's worth asking yourself: What really matters to *me*?

Who are you, really? Not just your parents' kid, or the person your friends know from group chats. What do you believe in? What makes you think, "Nope, not okay," or "Yes, this feels right"? Figuring that out means understanding your values, and it's one of the most important things you'll ever do. Once you're aware of your values, you stop just reacting to the world—you start deciding how you want to show up in it.

WHAT ARE VALUES, ANYWAY?

Back in the 1980s, people on TV were always going on about "values." Usually, it was a sanctimonious senator or moralizing televangelist talking about "family values" or "real values." A lot of them later got caught cheating on their taxes, breaking commandments, or doing something gross. So "values" started to feel like a phony word used by phony people.

But eventually, I figured out that values aren't just campaign slogans or fundraising clickbait. They're the beliefs that guide how you live your life, how you treat people, and how you make decisions—like lines on a road at night, helping you move in the right direction even when you can't see everything ahead. It's worth figuring out what you value so the life you're building is one you actually believe in.

Most of us start out with the values handed down to us by parents, families, or communities.

But growing up means questioning them as you take responsibility for your own life and actions. Do these beliefs feel true to you? Do they align with the kind of person you want to be and the life you want to live?

Values are personal, and yours don't have to match anyone else's. Some people hold onto beliefs that seem right to them but can actually cause harm. Those beliefs are usually rooted in how people were raised, the environment they live in, or personal experiences they've interpreted in a certain way. Often, these people genuinely believe they're doing the right thing based on their understanding of the world.

This is why it's so important to examine your beliefs as you change and grow. Are they based on facts, empathy, and fairness? Do they consider the common good? Or are they rooted in fear, misunderstanding, or bigotry?

Understanding your values—and ensuring they align with truth and goodness—helps you make thoughtful decisions, treat others with respect, and navigate life with integrity.

QUESTIONING WHAT YOU'VE LEARNED

Examining your beliefs takes effort. Sometimes people cling to harmful ideas just because those ideas have "always been that way." Take left-handedness. Centuries ago, someone just decided that being left-handed was a moral defect—that the left hand was controlled by the devil. Left-handed kids were punished and forced to write with their right hand. By the 1960s and '70s, science showed that left-handedness is natural and making people change was unfair and harmful. What changed? People finally listened more to facts than superstition, questioned an outdated belief, and proved it wrong. As a left-handed person, I'm so glad they did.

This should make you wonder: What outdated "truths" are still floating around today? Maybe a relative says something unkind about a group of people. Maybe a post or clip makes you stop and think, “Wait, is that actually true?” Your values come into play here—asking questions, checking the facts, and staying curious.

HOW VALUES SHOW UP IN EVERYDAY LIFE

Values aren’t abstract ideas—they’re in the choices you make every day. Have you ever noticed someone sitting alone at lunch and thought about joining them but worried what your friends might say? Or maybe a restaurant server got your order wrong—were you rude, or kind?

These are moments where your values show up, or don’t. If your actions align with what you believe, that’s so cool—thank you for living those values. If they don’t, it’s a chance to look at where your actions and values might be clashing. You always have the opportunity to do better next time.

Sometimes, it is easy to see where actions and values clash. If you value honesty, you probably know not to steal money out of someone's wallet. If you value being polite, you wouldn't clip your toenails in the middle seat of an airplane. But sticking to your values isn't always easy, especially when circumstances challenge them. Imagine you have strep throat, but it's your best friend's birthday party. You want to go, but showing up means infecting others. If you value health and integrity, you stay home—no matter how much it sucks. If you choose to go anyway, that's compromising your values.

When your actions line up with your beliefs, you strengthen your self-respect and earn your own trust. That's how you build integrity and genuine self-confidence.

STAYING TRUE TO YOURSELF

Peer pressure is real. Most people have a natural yearning for social belonging, and the desire to fit in can make you second-guess your instincts.

At some point, you'll face a situation where you have to decide: Do I stick with what feels right, or go along with everyone else?

Maybe someone's pushing you to send a selfie you're not comfortable sharing. Maybe friends are piling on a classmate online and it feels wrong to join in. If something makes you uneasy, that's a sign it goes against your values. Pay attention to that.

Standing up for what's right—especially when it's unpopular—takes courage. But those moments are chances to choose who you are and who you want to be.

EVOLVING BELIEFS

Your values can grow and change as you learn more about the world. This might happen through learning about new scientific discoveries, understanding different ideologies, or hearing from people whose lives are nothing like yours. Maybe it's a conversation with your best friend's dad, a human rights lawyer, that opens your eyes to what refugees endure. Or your camp counselor shares what it's like to live as an amputee. Sometimes it's quieter—a moment when something just feels off. Maybe you stumble across an Internet post of someone proudly posing next to a giraffe they've shot and think, *How is that fun for anyone?*

Learning about experiences outside your own doesn't just teach you—it shapes you.

Think of it like keeping your phone updated. You wouldn't stick with an outdated operating system full of bugs and glitches. Similarly, your beliefs need to evolve when better information comes along. You're not erasing the past—you're building on it with a clearer, more informed perspective.

YOUR VALUES IN ACTION

Here's the real test: How do you treat people? How do your actions align with what you say you believe?

It's one thing to say you value kindness and honesty. It's another to live those values when no one's watching. If you see someone being mistreated, do you speak up? If a friend shares something personal, do you keep it private? Your choices shape your integrity, your confidence, and the trust you have in yourself.

When you act on your values—even when it's hard—you build a foundation of self-respect. You know who you are. You know what you stand for. And that's a powerful way to live.

Pay attention to what feels right to you. Then act like it.

Experts view the five values below as the building blocks for all other values. Take a look at these to get started:

INTEGRITY: Being honest and consistent in your words and actions, even when it's tough; staying true to yourself and others.

RESPECT: Acknowledging the worth of every person, treating them as you'd like to be treated, and embracing differences without judgment.

RESPONSIBILITY: Taking ownership of your actions, decisions, and their outcomes; being accountable for mistakes and committing to making things right.

EMPATHY: Understanding and sharing the feelings of others. Empathy is the foundation for kindness, compassion, and mutual understanding.

COURAGE: Confronting challenges and fears, standing up for your beliefs, and doing what's right even when faced with difficulties.

DIGGING INTO YOUR VALUES

One of the best ways to identify your values is by going over the moments when you felt the most **you**—confident and proud. These moments often reveal what's important to you. These questions are similar to the prompt in Chapter 1, but this time, concentrate on the idea of values as you answer.

Identify the times when you were happiest.

- Think of a time when you felt genuinely joyful or at peace.
- What were you doing? Was it a solo activity, or were others involved?
- Who were you with, and how did their presence influence your happiness?
- Were there specific circumstances—like nature, music, or a sense of accomplishment—that contributed to that moment?

Step 2

Identify the times when you were most proud of yourself.

- What did you do that made you feel proud?
- Was it a personal achievement, standing up for someone, or helping others?
- Why did this moment feel significant? What values were you honoring?

Step 3

Identify the times when you were undoubtedly fulfilled and satisfied.

- Think of a time when you felt deeply content—like something had clicked.
- What need or desire was fulfilled in that moment?
- Was it about progress, connection, creativity, or something else?

Now review the moments you wrote down. What stands out to you? Do these experiences suggest values you live by—perhaps without even realizing it?

Once you've thought about these experiences, look for the overlap among happiness, pride, and fulfillment. These patterns point to your core values.

For example:

- If your happiest and proudest moments involved helping others, generosity or compassion might be a core value.
- If you feel most fulfilled while creating art, creativity or self-expression might be essential to who you are.

What three to five values emerge from this exercise?

NAME YOUR HEROES

Heroes and role models are like guides—they show us what we aspire to and highlight the strengths we value most. By identifying the people you admire and why, you can discover the values that resonate with you on a deeper level.

Identify and write down four people you look up to. Think of people who make you say, "I want to be like that." These could be family members, friends, public figures, or fictional characters.

Step 2

Define the values you admire in them. For each person, ask yourself:

- What makes them a hero to you? Is it their courage? Honesty? Humor? Perseverance?
- How do they show those values in their actions?

Here are some examples of people I admire:

- **Chappell Roan:** For the unapologetic way she embraces her identity and the sense of fun and theatricality she brings to her music. She makes it clear that being yourself—boldly and proudly—is a strength.
- **Fannie Lou Hamer:** Her courage and testimony brought attention to racial injustice, even after she was beaten by white supremacists for her activism. She fought for civil rights, voting rights, and better living conditions for marginalized communities—and she never gave up.
- **My friend Emmy:** She is funny, open-minded, and deeply committed to public service. She works to make the world fairer by championing diverse representation in politics and decision-making.
- **Lily Tomlin:** She's one of those amazing people who uses comedy to shift how people see the

world and each other. When I was in high school, I saw her one-woman show *The Search for Signs of Intelligent Life in the Universe*, and it totally expanded the way I thought about humor, the world, and even myself.

Think about your list. The values you see in your heroes often reveal what you care about most. Ask yourself:

- What do these values say about what's important to you? Are there any recurring themes?
- Do you admire these values because you already have them or because you aspire to develop them?
- Are there ways you already live out these values in your life?
- What small steps could you take to further develop these qualities in yourself?

Write down the three to five values you identified through your heroes.

WHAT VALUES RESONATE WITH YOU?

Now that you've spent time thinking about your experiences and your heroes, it's time to identify the values that feel most true to you. This exercise helps you see what you already have, what you want to develop, and what kind of world you want to live in.

Identify your values. At this point, you should have identified at least three to five values you see in yourself and your heroes. Compare that list to the list below. Do you see other values you already try to live by? Add those to your written list.

- **Honesty:** Being real and truthful even when it's uncomfortable.
- **Curiosity:** Being open to new ideas and asking questions.
- **Compassion:** Caring about what other people are going through.

- **Loyalty:** Showing up for the people you care about.
- **Independence:** Thinking for yourself and making your own choices.
- **Patience:** Knowing some things take time and being okay with that.
- **Humor:** Finding moments to laugh, even when things are hard.
- **Empathy:** Trying to understand how someone else feels and why it matters.
- **Courage:** Doing the right thing, even when it's scary or unpopular.
- **Justice:** Believing everyone deserves dignity, fairness, and the chance to live safely and freely.
- **Creativity:** Finding new ways to express yourself or solve a problem.
- **Inclusivity:** Making space for different people and experiences.
- **Kindness:** Being good to people on purpose.
- **Sustainability:** Taking care of the planet like your future depends on it (because it does)

Step 2

Using a different color in your notebook, circle the values in your list that you admire but want to work on in yourself. For example, maybe you want to be more patient or courageous in challenging situations.

- What did you do that made you feel proud?
- Was it a personal achievement, standing up for someone, or helping others?
- Why did this moment feel significant? What values were you honoring?

Step 3

In another color, circle or add to the list the values you believe the world needs more of—values you want to see championed in society.

After you've done that, look at the three categories of values you've highlighted: the values you already have, the values you're striving for, and the values you want to see in the world.

Your answers create a road map to understanding yourself:

- **The values you already live by are your strengths.** Appreciate those.
- **The values you want to develop show your growth potential.** Start small and look for ways to practice them in your everyday life.
- **The values you want to see in the world highlight your vision for a better future.** These point to causes you can stand behind and advocate for.

BONUS: Write down your top five values and keep them somewhere visible or type them into your phone notes. Look at them once a week and let them be your guide.

P

CHAPTER 4

Purpose Over Passion

ind your passion!"

"Pursue your passion!"

"LIVE YOUR PASSION!"

Every time I see Instagram posts like that, I can't help but think, *Please stop*. Instead of feeling inspired, I feel overwhelmed. And honestly, the word "passion" bums me out sometimes. Maybe it's because it makes me think of a trashy romance novel, or maybe it's because it seems overhyped. Maybe the idea of passion just doesn't resonate with everyone. While passion can be a powerful motivator, it isn't the only path to a fulfilling life.

There is so much emphasis on finding your passion that it can feel like you're falling behind if you haven't figured it all out yet. What if you don't have a burning interest in anything, really? Or what if your passions don't translate into a money-making career or side hustle? These are normal questions, and it's okay not to have the answers right now.

Passion is just an intense enthusiasm for something. You might feel passionate about a lot of things—astronomy, hoop dancing, nail art, Zydeco music, or fixing cars. Or maybe you are looking into different interests but haven't landed on anything specific yet. That's completely fine.

But beyond passion, there's something deeper: your sense of purpose. While passion is often tied to specific activities, purpose answers a bigger question: *Why?* It's the connection between your values, talents, and experiences—a thread that gives meaning to what you do.

Purpose channels your energy toward something bigger than yourself. For example, if you love creating art, your purpose might be helping others see the world through new viewpoints. If you value knowledge, your purpose could involve inspiring others to stay informed. Or if you're driven to alleviate suffering, your purpose might be rooted in advocacy and compassion.

Passion and purpose don't have to compete—they can complement each other. Let's say you're passionate about playing the banjo. You practice because you like it and it feels satisfying and you feel kind of cool and enjoy being able to do it.

Purpose takes that enthusiasm and adds direction, like becoming a professional in a bluegrass band, teaching banjo lessons at a retirement center, or playing for charity events. Purpose adds depth, turning a personal interest into something that benefits yourself or others.

This process takes time. Purpose doesn't drop into your lap fully formed; it grows through experiences and self-observation. It usually begins as a spark—an interest with some *oomph* behind it. For me, it started with a film class I took in college when I was nineteen. We watched *Eyes on the Prize*, a documentary about the fight civil rights movement. Watching everyday people risk everything just to be treated fairly hit me hard and it stayed with me. Some things change how you see the world, and this was one of those things. It made me start paying closer attention.

That was a lightbulb moment for me and I felt pulled toward journalism because when the news is done well, it helps people understand what's really going on. Solid reporting can shine a light on issues, policies, and choices that shape lives. I wanted to be part of that. I wanted to help bring real experiences into the open, so more people could see what life is like for someone living a different reality than their own. When people understand what others are actually dealing with, they're more likely to care and maybe even rethink their perspective.

Noticing what makes you pay attention is where it begins. These lightbulb moments can tell you something. Take note of them, because they can point you toward something meaningful that can give your life direction.

OVERCOMING BARRIERS

Purpose isn't always easy to uncover, especially for those with limited access to resources. In many underserved communities, systemic barriers like poverty and discrimination can make it harder to explore aspirations for the future. Everyone deserves the chance to discover their unique gifts, and if you're navigating these challenges, know that it's still possible to uncover what matters to you.

Local libraries, community centers, and free online tools can be powerful starting points. Seek out mentors—teachers, coaches, or family members—who can guide and encourage you. Volunteering, joining clubs, or attending workshops can be your entry to new interests and skills.

Malala Yousafzai was just a teenager when the Taliban tried to silence her for wanting an education. In her part of Pakistan, girls weren't allowed to go to school, and speaking out against that was dangerous. She spoke out against it anyway, describing what life was like under Taliban rule and why it was wrong to deny girls an education. The Taliban tried to scare her and did everything they could to stop her, but she would not be stopped. Her sense of purpose came from championing education as a human right. Malala has greatly influenced global education policies, especially girls' access to education. She is a great example of how connecting values to action can create real change.

CULTIVATING CURIOSITY

Living with purpose doesn't have to feel like an overwhelming responsibility. It doesn't need to start with a grand mission or a world-changing goal. Start small. Let your curiosity guide you. Explore new interests, think about what excites or concerns you, and notice the issues that catch your attention.

What kind of world do you want to help create? What problems do you care about solving?

The more you learn about yourself and your surroundings, the clearer your purpose will become.

Maybe you realize you want to help others feel less lonely. Maybe you really like yourself when you're taking care of shelter animals. Purpose comes from a process of discovery. Those revelations are stepping stones toward living out your sense of purpose.

I've said it before, and I'll say it again because it's important: You don't need to have it all figured out right now. There's so much to do or to fix in the world that you might feel called toward many purposes! For now, pick one purpose to focus on and know that you can explore others as you go.

BUILDING A LIFE OF PURPOSE

Once you've identified a purpose, get involved with people and causes that align with it. Talk to others who share your interests, join communities online or in person, and volunteer for organizations that are already taking action. You'll meet like-minded people, see things in a new way, and discover even more ways to contribute.

Purpose isn't static—it develops as you do. It grows with your experiences, changes with your priorities, and adapts to new stages of life. The through-line is your commitment to living in a way that matches your values and leaves the world a little better than you found it.

Every experience adds to your story. Whether you're helping a neighbor, learning a new skill, or standing up for something you believe in, you're shaping a purposeful life. Keep showing up with curiosity and sincerity. The shape of your purpose will reveal itself over time, not as a destination but as a way of being.

Nurture your passions, but let purpose be the steady glow that guides your journey. The world needs what only you can offer, and every small step you take toward a meaningful life makes a difference.

WHAT'S IMPORTANT TO ME?

Ask yourself the following questions. Once you've answered them, interview someone you admire and aspire to be like. Ask them the same questions.

What are the three most important subjects of your life?

How did you discover that you cared about those things?

What does it mean to have a good life and be a good person?

What gives your life meaning at this moment?

If you were looking back on your life, how would you want to be remembered?

Compare your answers with the person you've interviewed, and pay attention to the similarities and differences. How do their answers make you feel? Does their perspective influence how you think about your own? Are there shared values or purposes between you? Are there differences that inspire you to think about life in new ways?

Ask yourself: Are my current actions and choices aligning with what I say is most important to me? If not, how might I start shifting things to bring my day-to-day life closer to my ideas of purpose and fulfillment?

INSIGHTS FROM FUTURE YOU

Close your eyes and imagine yourself as a wise eighty-year-old. Things in your life and the world have gone as well as you could have hoped. Take your time envisioning the following details:

- Who will be in your life? These could be people you know now or figures you have yet to meet, like roommates, a partner, or children.
- Where is home, and who is sharing it with you?
- Do you have pets?
- If you're retired, what work did you do?
- What communities are you a part of?
- How have you helped or changed the world—or at least a small part of it?
- How do you stay creative or contribute now?

Spend several minutes imagining your best possible future, then write in your journal for ten to fifteen minutes about what you envisioned.

Later, review what you've written, and pay attention to what stands out most. Are there specific relationships, values, or ideas that shape your vision? Which emotions came up while imagining this future—joy, pride, contentment? Even some unease?

Ask yourself: Are there ways I can start working toward this best future now? Look for gaps between your future vision and your current reality. For example, if you imagine yourself remembered for making positive contributions to a cause that matters to you, consider how you might start participating.

F
F
F
F
F

CHAPTER 5

Failure Is Fine

I know what failure feels like. My freshman year of college at Sewanee hit me like a wrecking ball—emotionally, academically, physically. I started off optimistic, but by second semester I was completely overwhelmed. I couldn't keep up with deadlines, I wasn't sleeping enough, and my confidence was shot. I felt like I was failing at everything.

Then came the letter from the Dean's office. Not a good letter.

My grades were so bad, it said, that I would need to get my act together somewhere else in order to be allowed back. If I wanted another shot at Sewanee, I had to get excellent grades elsewhere first.

So, I spent a semester in my hometown at the University of Houston. My friend Jon calls that stretch of time my "semester abroad." It's funny now, but back then there was nothing funny about it. I felt ashamed, embarrassed, and convinced that I had thrown my life off course.

My sense of failure was about more than bad grades. It felt like I had failed as a person—like

I wasn't who I thought I was. A good student. A responsible adult. Someone who deserved the sacrifices my parents made to pay for college. My self-regard hit an all-time low.

I gave myself no grace at all. The way I was talking to myself could've been its own podcast: *How to Make It Worse.*

I've destroyed my future.

I'm a complete failure.

I am a loser and will never get on the right track.

The situation was really about a lot more than challenging academics. I was lost and didn't have the tools to deal with it. Maybe failing was my mind's way of saying, *This is too much, and I don't know what to do.*

Thankfully, things changed—but not overnight. It took time. I worked hard, studied intensely, and put in the effort to gain respect for myself. After a semester of straight A's at U of H, I was able to go back to Sewanee. I hoped to be someone who could learn from her mistakes. And I did. By senior year, I had made up for lost time. I had all the credits I needed to graduate, I wrote for the school newspaper, and I had formed a group of smart, funny friends.

Missing one semester was not the end of the world after all. More importantly, I proved to myself that I could recover from failure. Failure doesn't define you unless you let it. I also learned that failure wasn't the real enemy, my shame was.

If you're carrying shame over a setback, remember: It's just one chapter, not the entire story. You don't have to punish yourself to move forward. Learning to be kind to yourself, *especially* when you feel like you've blown it, is what actually helps you find the will to get over it and try again.

One day, you'll be able to look back and say, "That was rough, but I made it through." And you will. With time, I came to see my Sewanee experience not just as a failure, but as a wake-up call. It showed me how hard I was on myself—and how perfectionism can turn every mistake into a crisis. I didn't need to be flawless. I needed to learn from mistakes and setbacks and think of it as building up my bank of experiences.

PERFECTIONISM AND THE FEAR OF FAILURE

Perfectionism is the fear of not being good enough. It pressures you to strive for flawlessness—an impossible standard. Fear of failure is amplified by perfectionism because any mistake or setback feels like a catastrophe, which can suck away your energy and drive. And it's not just emotionally draining—research shows that this kind of relentless self-pressure is closely tied to anxiety and depression. Perfectionism tricks you into thinking you need to avoid failure at all costs.

The irony is that perfectionism always fails. You WILL mess up in some way, because you're human, as is everyone else on earth. And when that happens, perfectionism doesn't protect you from failure; it just makes failure feel unbearable.

This personality trait doesn't come out of nowhere. Teen girls pick up messages from all around them that they need to be perfect, that to have worth they need to excel academically, thrive socially, and meet trending beauty standards. Society praises boys for being tough, while girls are praised for their appearance, people-pleasing skills, and being easygoing.

Think of social media: It's easy to scroll through carefully curated feeds and feel like everyone else's life is better than yours. But behind every filtered image or post about an amazing life is an imperfect person with their own struggles. Comparing yourself to those highlight reels can lead to harsh self-criticism. But you aren't missing anything. You are wonderful just as you are. What you don't have is a ring light, wind machine, makeup artist, hair extensions, and a ton of fillers.

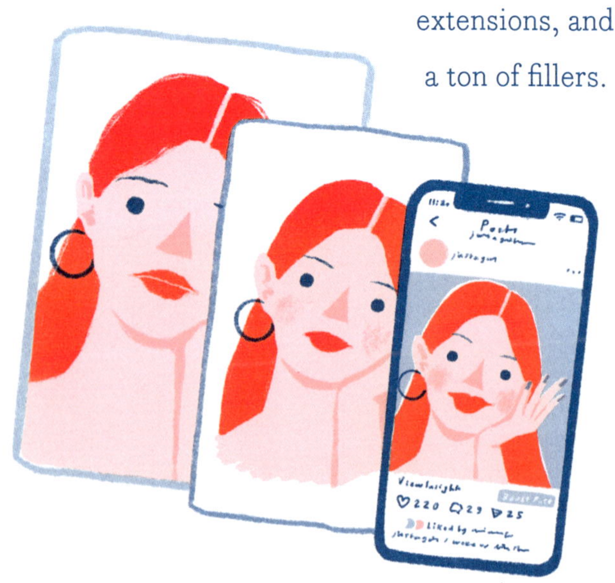

Your value and worth aren't something to be gained by being perfect or doing everything flawlessly. Your value just is. It's there from the very start. It is built in. It is inherent. And it doesn't come from external achievements. You don't need to earn it through perfection. Take a deep breath and realize you don't have to even try to be perfect. Real progress comes when you give yourself permission to mess up, do your best to learn from it, and keep going. If you let the fear of not being perfect hold you back, you risk losing out on discovering what makes you truly unique.

When you catch yourself spiraling into self-doubt or comparison, try to keep this in mind: *Nobody gets it right all of the time.* Imperfection is what's normal. Beyoncé tripped during one of her performances. Simone Biles has wobbled on the balance beam. Dolly Parton... Okay, wait, maybe there is *one* perfect person.

Back to the point: no one enjoys screwing up. It's natural to fear failure. But you have a choice in how you view these moments. You can treat failure like a full-blown identity crisis, or you can see it for what it is, a learning tool. The second option serves you way better because taking risks, tripping, wobbling, and learning as you go is how you become independent and interesting.

Let's establish this truth: failing at something does not mean you are a failure. It's easy to confuse the two, especially when the voice in your head whispers, "Way to go! You're a loser!" But that's not true. Failure isn't a declaration; it's a signal that you're still learning and trying.

FEAR OF FAILURE

So, why do people freak out about failing? It's more than just the act of messing up—it's all the what-ifs that come with it. *What if people think I'm a loser? What if I disappoint my family or friends? What if I embarrass myself?*

The toughest failures are moral ones: the failure to live up to our own moral compass. These *aren't* stories we laugh about later: Blowing off plans with a friend going through a breakup. Not visiting your grandmother at the nursing home. Talking behind someone's back. Laughing at a racist joke because you want people to think you're easygoing. Not preparing for and failing a test is one thing, but not living according to what's important to you and your values feels much worse and can haunt you for years. These failures are a bigger deal because they affect how much or how little we like ourselves, staying with us and challenging our self-image: *Am I really a good person? A good friend?* They add up if we don't catch them and do the work of not repeating them.

The way to repair after those kinds of failures is to take responsibility, learn the lesson, and strive to do better. Moral failures aren't final, but they are tough lessons in who we are and who we want to become.

THE POWER OF SELF-COMPASSION

One way to combat fear of failure, perfectionism, and harsh self-criticism is to learn to be more self-compassionate. Failure stings, no doubt about it. It can send you into a spiral of gloomy discouragement. The good news is, self-compassion is a tool for responding to these moments, as it teaches you to treat yourself with kindness and give yourself some nurturing support.

When you mess up, you usually have a choice: you can pile on the blame, or you can treat yourself like a friend who needs encouragement. Instead of saying, "I'm a failure," try, "Okay, I really messed up this time. Let's figure out what went wrong and how to do better." That shift in mindset takes practice, but it can be life changing. You can learn how to start that practice right here, right now.

1 Pay attention to your feelings.

As I've said throughout this book, noticing and naming your feelings is the first step toward handling them in a healthy way. Don't retreat from them but do get better at them. Find the right balance of honesty, acceptance, and kindness toward yourself.

2 Understand that everyone flops and fumbles and it's a normal part of being human.

3 Practice positive self-talk.

Instead of trash-talking yourself, try saying, "I'm not proud of what I did, but there's no reason to be mean to myself. I'll do better next time." Then try to stop thinking about it. When you do this, be sure to use *realistic* positive self-talk. You want to believe what you are saying, and if you're feeling really crappy, repeating "I AM THE GREATEST!" probably won't help. But a simple, true affirmation can make a difference in how you feel. The sentences on the next page offer more examples of reframing your experiences so you can move forward.

Self-Compassion Phrases to Practice

"My mistakes do not define me. They refine me."

"It is okay to mess up. How I handle that is up to me."

"I forgive myself for what I did while I was learning."

"I'm not where I want to be yet, and that's okay."

"I messed up big-time, but if I choose to learn from it, it won't be for nothing."

"These stitches in my forehead are a strong conversation starter!"

What would you add to this list?

These aren't magic words, but they can help. Think of them as the kind of things you'd say to a friend, but instead you're saying them to yourself.

Training your brain so that your first response to a mistake is "I'll figure this out" takes work and doesn't come easy. Like many things in life, you must learn how to do it and keep practicing.

TAKING CHANCES OUTSIDE OF THE ZONE OF COMFORT

The temptation to stay comfortable can hold you back. You've probably heard the age-old advice that you need to "get out of your comfort zone." In real terms, that means that most of the time, people do what feels familiar. Doing what you already know you are capable of—the tried and true—feels comfortable and safe. But keeping yourself at Level One instead of feeling like a bumbler at Level Two means you're staying stuck at Level One. Don't just stick with what you know. Stretch and try and reach and attempt. Try new levels outside the zone of comfort.

Striking a balance between what's comfortable and exploring new zones is a major part of becoming the person you want to be. The more of this you do, the more you'll start to like being in your own company. You become more interesting to yourself. You'll know you're the kind of person who tries things and is willing to put up with some discomfort or failure to break through to the next stage.

When you try something new, there's no way it will be perfect, and it will most likely entail some slight mortification and/or total flops. Good! Those conditions can end up creating some of the funniest stories of our lives. Who among us hasn't needed stitches the first time they touched a surfboard? Okay, maybe that's just me. But at least I cracked my head open in front of the maximum number of people I wanted to impress!

Learning to handle failure with the right attitude is essential, because there is no way to avoid failure in life. The scope and size of your failure can vary, but it's definitely going to happen. The difference between it becoming a gigantic marker of your life or just a blip where you learned something is all in your attitude. I mean, you *can* choose to take on a new identity, move towns, and start a new life to get over it . . . or you could use some self-soothing talk or conversations with people who love you to ride out your initial reaction, figure out what happened, and decide what you can learn from it. My go-to when I've screwed up is a reframe. I shift my perspective. Instead of seeing failure as evidence that I'm terrible, I see it as proof that I am learning, trying, and evolving. Which one would you prefer?

The most interesting people aren't those who never fail; they're the ones who learn to fail better next time, to talk to themselves tenderly about it, and to use their setbacks as stepping stones to the next thing. Go forth and dare to be imperfect, to stumble, and to learn more about yourself.

How to Learn from Failure

Acknowledge Your Feelings

Give yourself time to process your emotions. Feeling disappointed or frustrated is okay; just try not to dwell there for too long.

Analyze the Situation

What went wrong? Was it a bad decision, or something outside of your control?

Consider Different Perspectives

Try to see the situation from others' viewpoints. Would they regard this as a failure? Why or why not?

Identify Lessons Learned

What could have been done differently here? What can you do differently next time? Be specific.

Reframe Your Mindset

Instead of viewing failure as purely negative, see it as a stop along the way to getting where you want to go.

LEAVING THE ZONE OF COMFORT AND FAMILIARITY

Think about all of the new things you have experienced over the last year. These could be tasting different foods, hanging out with new friends, or trying activities you hadn't done before. Pick three experiences and answer the questions below.

1. What happened when you tried it?

2. What did you struggle with? What went wrong? What went right? Did the benefits outweigh the struggles?

3. If you made any mistakes here, how did you handle them?

4. What did you learn about yourself? What personal strengths emerged? What fears or limiting beliefs were challenged?

5. What did you gain from the experience? How has it shaped your willingness to take on future challenges?

Look for patterns in your answers that highlight your adaptability, areas where you might still need to push further, and the rewards that come from taking risks.

TALKING TO YOURSELF IS HIGHLY ENCOURAGED

Imagine your best friend is telling you about something she screwed up: She stayed up late scrolling TikTok, didn't study at all for her test, and totally bombed it. She feels stupid and embarrassed. What would you say to your friend?

1. Consider how you'd counsel your friend here. What comfort would you give? What forward movement would you offer?

2. In contrast, think about when you last let yourself down. Note what you typically say to yourself—the words, actions, and tone.

3. Imagine treating yourself as kindly as you treat your friend. Write down how things could change if you extended the same kindness to yourself during tough times.

The way you speak to yourself during difficult moments can make a big difference in your ability to recover and get over it. By comparing how you treat your friends versus yourself, you can identify areas where self-compassion might be missing. This practice can guide you toward more constructive and supportive self-talk.

WHAT "SUCCESS" LOOKS LIKE
HELPING PEOPLE IN NEED
HAVING MEANINGFUL EXPERIENCE AND TRUE FRIENDSHIPS
LIVING ACCORDING TO VALUES
DEVELOPING GOOD CHARACTER
MAKING CHOICES THAT BUILD SELF-RESPECT
BEING INDEPENDEN

CHAPTER 6

Success? Says Who?

Society loves to measure worth by achievements—job titles, awards, follower counts. The messaging is relentless. From a young age, we're fed the same script: Work hard, follow the path, achieve more. For some, this roadmap offers comfort and direction. For others, it feels suffocating, like a script someone else wrote for their life. Wherever you land, it's worth pressing pause and asking: *What do I* actually *want? What feels right for me?*

The world is loud with opinions about success—how much money you make, how impressive your title is, or what the "perfect" life looks like. But success doesn't follow one general script.

It's personal. It's shaped by your values, your aspirations, your definition of what matters most. Your version of a fulfilling life might look nothing like someone else's—and that's not only okay, it's good.

And it would be fair and good if everyone started the race for success on a level playing field. But that isn't how it is. Systemic barriers like racism, sexism, and xenophobia create uneven starting lines. Some of us have doors opened for us—through luck, privilege, or timing—while others face challenges that make those same opportunities harder to reach. My own path to where I am today has been a mix of opportunities I was fortunate enough to stumble into, odd jobs I didn't love, missteps I learned from, and moments I wouldn't trade for anything. But I know that isn't everyone's story.

Acknowledging our past challenges doesn't take away the value of hard work; it deepens it. It pushes us to rethink how we have achieved success—not via someone else's checklist, but through a life rich with meaning, connection, and moments of joy, even in the face of obstacles. Recognizing systemic unfairness also reminds us of the bigger picture: we can appreciate our own progress while also advocating for a world where more people have the chance to thrive.

Your worth isn't earned—it's something you already have. The question isn't *How do I measure up to others?* but *What kind of life do I want to create for myself?*

A CHANGING CONVERSATION

Every day, younger generations are rewriting the rules of success. Gen Z and Gen Alpha grasp the idea that some people do what they love for a living, while others find meaning and purpose outside of work. Young people like you are prioritizing mental health over burnout, individuality over conformity, and purpose over pressure. You all know that there are a lot of powerful, ultra-wealthy people who are miserable. There's a shift toward living well instead of chasing the hustle, and honestly, we elders could take a few notes.

Success today doesn't have to center on a job title or a paycheck. Many people find purpose in their hobbies, relationships, and communities, whether or not their day job makes a ton of money or aligns with their passions. Think of the introductions on *The Great British Bake-Off*: "Safika is a bus driver in Surrey who restores antique clocks, grows heirloom tomatoes, sings in her community choir, and took up baking during the pandemic." That life sounds rich, doesn't it? Compare it to something like, "Toby is a CEO who drives a Tesla and watches Fox News in his spare time." Safika's life satisfaction comes from cultivating hobbies, relationships, and purpose beyond her paycheck, and to me, at least, that feels more like real success.

THE VALUE OF EXPLORATION

Not long ago, I asked a high school senior what she wanted to do after graduation. She smiled and thanked me for not asking the the usual questions like "Where are you going to college?" or "What's your major?" For a moment, she felt seen as a whole person, not just a decision about a school or subject. She didn't have an answer yet, and it was cool to listen to her thoughts about it. The process of exploring (trying things, messing up, figuring it out) is how you actually find your way.

My own exploratory time was full of random jobs and unexpected lessons. I've been a law firm file clerk, a cater waiter, a retail worker, and even a rose de-thorner. The boring jobs, the tough jobs, the "What am I doing here?" jobs—they became building blocks for my future because each one taught me something valuable. The law firm showed me I wasn't comfortable supporting lawyers who denied injured workers fair compensation. When I worked as a cook, I discovered how much I love making food for others, and picked up some useful skills along the way. From being a hostess and receptionist, I developed people skills: how to problem-solve, calm someone down, and have comfortable conversations with strangers. Sometimes the job itself matters less than the people you work with, the skills you pick up, or the questions you grapple with. All of them offer the chance to figure out more about yourself and how you work best.

Okay, but what does it look like, exactly, to learn about yourself while you're working the late shift at the check-out register? It looks like living up to your personal values by approaching the job with integrity regardless of the task at hand. Working with integrity means doing your best with honesty and a strong sense of responsibility and taking pride in your work. Even if it's your first job, you can find ways to feel good about your work. Maybe you can perfect your sweater-folding technique or help another new coworker through their first shift. Small actions and choices make a big difference over time about how you regard yourself.

GRATITUDE AS A PERSPECTIVE SHIFT

Sometimes it feels like you're supposed to have your whole life figured out already. The pressure to achieve comes from all directions—school counselors asking about your five-year plan, friends who picked a college major, TikTokkers announcing scholarships or "dream job" wins. And even the people who care about you most can accidentally make it worse. Their advice often sounds like *"Please make choices that help ME feel less freaked out about your future."*

When that stress builds, gratitude can be a powerful way to regain perspective. Yes, it's a concept that has become something of a cliché, but gratitude is a powerful way to manage stress and shift your point of view. Maybe thinking of it as *appreciation* makes more sense to you. Practicing gratitude doesn't mean ignoring the tough stuff or pretending to feel great when you really just want to cry by yourself. It means noticing the good things that are often overlooked while you're busy stressing about everything else.

I admit that ever since I've started practicing gratitude, I tend to sound a lot like Buddy the elf from the movie *Elf*: "Good news, I saw a dog today!"

When I'm in the shower on very cold days, I say out loud, "THANK YOU FOR THIS HOT SHOWER!" Appreciation cheers me up and helps me see what's going my way.

Research shows that gratitude actually rewires your brain: When you notice something good, you stimulate the ventromedial prefrontal cortex, which is part of the brain's reward circuitry. That stimulation causes you to feel calmer, more patient, more generous, and also less materialistic.

In order to practice gratitude, look around at what's right in front of you—but also let your mind wander. You might be thankful for the fruits you love to eat, and then you can be grateful to the people who picked those fruits. If you're sick, you might really appreciate antibiotics and a cozy bed. Gratitude could be as simple as appreciating a sweet text or a bright full moon at night that looks really cool.

You can find things to be grateful for by asking yourself these questions:

1. What went well for me this week?
2. What things at home make me feel comfortable or make life a little easier?
3. Who makes me laugh? Who do I have fun hanging out with?

Finding goodness in everyday moments turns ordinary life into successful living. All you have to do is decide to notice.

LIVING YOUR VERSION OF SUCCESS

What does it mean to live a successful life?

For me, it's things like laughing a lot, knowing what's right and wrong (and trying to act like it), helping lost dogs find their people, surrounding myself with smart, funny friends, loving the people in my life and letting them love me back . . . and doing what I can to squash unfairness when I see it. To me, those feel more fulfilling than any award.

One of the moments I'm proudest of had nothing to do with recognition. It came from a stray dog. She was skittish, thin, and abandoned. Most people saw her and went on their way, assuming she wasn't their problem. But I couldn't do that.

So, I did what I could. I left food and water where she could find it, then slowly moved the food closer to my house, hoping to lead her away from the busier streets. Little by little, she followed. She wouldn't come inside my gate, but she started sleeping just outside of it. Then, one morning, she finally curled up in my yard and let me come near. That's when I saw her swollen eye and the way she limped when she stood. She was clearly in pain and needed help.

With the support of a few neighbors, we got her the medical care she needed. I posted in local adoption groups and message boards, sharing what a sweet girl she was. Two weeks later, after healing from surgery, she was adopted. I bawled my eyes out, relieved she had a safe, loving home. No award could ever top that feeling. Success!

Another time, I completed the New York City Marathon. I finished in 32,205th place and didn't even run the whole way. By most definitions, that's not success. But crossing the finish line felt like a win because I had trained for months just to be able to jog and walk for over five hours straight.

More than that, I got to experience New York

City in a way I never had before—traveling through every borough on foot, surrounded by cheering crowds shouting encouragement. And at the finish line, my friends were there jumping, yelping, and hugging me like I had won the whole thing. It was a wonderful day, and it taught me that success comes from showing up, following through, and finding meaning in what you do.

Success doesn't have to mean winning, dominating, or collecting titles and trophies. Success can look like knowing who you are and living in a way that feels good to you. No matter what, your idea of success can change over time, and it's yours to define as you go.

SHIFT YOUR FOCUS TO THE GOOD

If I asked you to name three things that are going wrong, you'd probably have an immediate answer: You didn't sleep well last night, your bangs are too short, and one of your friends is icing you out. But what if I asked you to name three things that are going well? You might have to stop and think.

So let's do that.

- Pause whatever you're doing.
- Shift your focus to something good that is in your life. It might be a pleasing little everyday thing—like a phone you can carry in your hand that beams to a satellite in space. Maybe at lunch, you and your friend laughed until your stomach hurt watching *Parks and Recreation* clips. There are people who pick up your garbage every week. There are birds singing in the trees. You have access to books that feed your brain. Pick one thing that makes your life better, safer, easier, or more fun.

- Keep your attention on that something good for at least ten to twenty seconds. If it's an object, picture yourself holding it and using it and the good you get from it. If it's a moment or an experience, relive it from start to finish. Allow yourself to fully appreciate it. Bask in the knowledge that there is something that feels good to have in your life.
- Try this exercise again with two more good things.

Write down the good things you appreciated during this exercise. How did it feel to focus on them? Did it bring a sense of calm or thankfulness? Could you make connections to other positive things in your life? Often, when we focus on one good thing, we begin to see many others we might have forgotten about. This practice shows how attention shapes perception—how what we focus on takes on weight and presence in our minds.

Consider how you can make this appreciation a practice in your daily life. The more you seek out and notice the good, the easier it becomes to see it, even on tough days.

SEE YOURSELF THROUGH FRESH EYES

Pretend you're a cosmic traveler from another galaxy. You land on Earth, step out of your spacepod, and start exploring. Everything is new and unfamiliar. What fascinates you? What captures your attention?

Now, imagine you walk into the house where the real you lives. Go into your room and look around as if you've never been there before:

What's in this space?

What do these things say about the person who lives here?

Who is this fascinating person?

What makes her interesting, cool, or unique?

Write these answers down, then consider what stood out to you about yourself. Did you notice qualities or interesting details you hadn't thought about recently? Are there talents, hobbies, or just cool things about yourself you may have been taking for granted?

This exercise helps you see yourself with fresh eyes and appreciate the wonderful person you already are. Keep this cosmic traveler's point of view in mind when self-doubt creeps in—it's easy to forget just how fascinating you are.

CHAPTER 7

Social Media: Scroll Smarter

Do you ever feel bad after hours of scrolling? Yes! Will you ever get to the end of your phone? No! This could go on forever. Your brain is taking in beauty tutorials, conspiracy theories, GRWMs, feuds, hot takes, and AI-generated weirdness. It's entertaining. It's addictive. And it's shaping how you see yourself, your worth, and what's considered "normal." Posts and TikToks start to feel like the standard for how you should look, what success means, even what kind of person you're supposed to be. It's a lot. Especially when truth seems to be optional and bad behavior is rewarded.

Well, don't worry, this chapter isn't here to tell you to quit. It's here to help you scroll smarter, think more critically, and stay in tune with who you are.

Maybe when you think about your social media, your main concerns are *How do I come across? Is anyone talking about me? What do people think of me?* It's natural to wonder about how people see you, but constantly checking, analyzing, and fretting about others' opinions can take a toll.

To add to all of that, YOU are also thinking of other people, talking about them, forming opinions, reacting to what their life looks like. Every time you open an app, you're hit with a wave of opinions, updates, comments, and photos. Sometimes it's fun. Sometimes it's serious. A lot of times it is overwhelming.

Now, some psychologists, behaviorists, and neurologists would say, "Please just log all the way off for a long time." But you probably won't do that. Instead, try taking short breaks every now and then to give your brain some time away from all that input. Make it a practice to ask yourself if what you are looking at makes you feel good or bad. Unfollow or mute accounts that don't add anything positive to your life. Remember that *you* are in control. You can follow or not follow, log in or log out.

Beyond the personal effects, remember that everything you post online—every comment, hot take, heart, or repost—feeds the social media machine. And sometimes, that "machine" does real harm. What if something you shared spreads false information? What if it hurt someone in real life? Cleaning up after that is way harder than avoiding making a mess in the first place.

Take the Springfield pet-eating lie. In September 2024, a single post on a Facebook group shared a rumor that Haitian immigrants in Springfield, Ohio, were stealing and eating pets. Anti-immigrant groups on social media went wild with the story, and even prominent figures like then-Senator J.D. Vance and President Trump pushed the lie. Law enforcement quickly confirmed there was absolutely no evidence of pet-stealing, and the person who started the rumor agreed and regretted posting about it at all—but the damage was done. The Haitian community faced harassment for weeks, and two elementary schools were evacuated and a middle school was closed after receiving bomb threats.

This shows how fast rumors, lies, and false information can spiral out of control, causing real-world harm. One post or repost can ripple outward in ways that are impossible to undo. The next time you're about to hit "share," pause and ask: *Could this post do harm? Am I contributing to the greater good or am I maybe part of the problem?*

It's wild (and depressing) how often people share false information online without realizing it. We've all been there in one way or another. Picture this: You see a post claiming Gracie Abrams and Bad Bunny are coming to your town for a surprise concert. Freaking out, you hit "Share" immediately. Then—surprise!—you find out it was a joke. But it's too late. Now your friends are mad at you for hyping them up, and you're embarrassed over how easily you fell for it.

Or maybe you're really into health and fitness, so you repost an influencer's "miracle detox drink" that promises to clear acne overnight. Your friend tries it, breaks out in a rash, and ends up at the dermatologist. How do you even apologize for something like that? You'd have to start by learning the lesson: Sharing scammy health claims, or *any* claims, without checking the facts can do more harm than good—and it's on you to double-check before spreading bad advice or outright lies.

SORTING TRUTH FROM LIES

Social media is a nonstop firehose of information. As Bo Burnham aptly put it: "Can I interest you in everything all of the time?" Some of what you see is trustworthy, a lot of it isn't. Lies, propaganda, misinformation, and disinformation flood your feed every second of every day. Here's a quick breakdown of these terms:

- **Lies** are deliberate falsehoods intended to deceive. *Example:* "Timothée Chalamet eats Jell-O at every meal."
- **Propaganda** pushes a one-sided narrative to influence opinions. *Example:* "Timothée Chalamet eats Jell-O at every meal—and we should all eat Jell-O to support our great American Jell-O manufacturers."
- **Misinformation** spreads false information unknowingly. *Example:* "Jell-O added to smoothies makes your hair grow and fights fungal infections."

- **Disinformation** is crafted to intentionally mislead or manipulate. *Example:* "Big Jell-O controls the weather."

Navigating this flood requires active effort. Before sharing, ask yourself:

- "Who benefits if I believe this?"
- "How does this make me feel, and does someone benefit if I feel this way?
- "Is there solid evidence to back this up?"

Sometimes, a little skepticism goes a long way. For example, "Why would an influencer DM me with a discount code?" or "Hang on, cats can't talk, right?" can keep you from going to a scammy website or making a fool of yourself in a video. These questions may seem obvious, but the principle applies to any claim: pause and think critically before you act.

More definitions: **Facts** are provable truths, like "Water boils at a hundred degrees Celsius," while **opinions** reflect personal beliefs, like "Stomach sleepers are evil—*and they want to teach stomach sleeping in schools!*" Blurring the line between fact and opinion can be dangerous. For example, if you repost someone denying that an impending hurricane is a threat, that opinion could put lives at risk if other people believe it. Sharing responsibly helps shape what others learn and how they act. Truth and accuracy make society sustainable.

SPOTTING BIAS AND AVOIDING TRAPS

Lies spread because people don't pause to think things through. Fact-checking, even for a moment, slows that roll. You can stop misinformation from going any further by analyzing claims, digging deeper, and evaluating the facts before sharing—and it's especially important to do that when something confirms what you want to believe.

Bias affects everyone. Following patterns is how your brain makes sense of the world—and it's also how misinformation sneaks past you. You're more likely to believe something if it matches what you already think, a pattern known as "confirmation bias." For example, someone who believes climate change isn't real might share a post saying "Climate Change is a Hoax" without noticing the sketchy source—like, say, the Russian State Propaganda Agency in Charge of Making People Doubt the Reality of Climate Change website.

To avoid these traps, challenge your assumptions. Ask:

- Who's behind this message? Who funds it, and who benefits from it?
- Does the author have the expertise to speak on this?
- Are they being transparent about facts and evidence?

Red flags are everywhere if you know how to catch them. If an article criticizing renewable energy comes from someone employed by an oil company, that is a blazing red flag for you to consider their motives. Similarly, if a wellness influencer on YouTube tells you to dismiss a Nobel Prize–winning epidemiologist about vaccine science, that's another red flag—especially if the influencer is selling "remedies" on her website. Being curious, asking questions, and evaluating sources makes you harder to manipulate and smarter about what you share.

High-quality news sources clearly distinguish between news and opinion, correct their errors publicly, and prioritize fact-checking. Scientific research is considered trustworthy when it comes from experts, is reviewed by other independent experts, and follows rigorous standards to ensure accuracy and fairness. Look for those practices as signs of trustworthiness and then verify information through multiple sources. Compare how different outlets report the same event, and challenge your built-in opinions by engaging with viewpoints that contradict your own.

Finally, watch out for clickbait. If a political post or headline makes you gasp—"WHAT?

Wildfires are caused by space lasers?!"—that's your cue to pause. Clickbait exists to rile you up and make you share before you think. Again, ask yourself: Who benefits from this story? Who could it harm?

The more you fact-check, the more control you have over what influences you. By sharing accurate information, you're protecting yourself and the people who see what you share. That makes you part of the solution, not the problem.

ACKNOWLEDGE THE DESIGN

Social media platforms are engineered to keep you scrolling. Ever searched for "striped shorts" and realized three hours later you're watching your twentieth video of people slipping and falling? That's by design. That is the business model. The longer you stay on an app, the more ads you see, and the more money tech companies make. Your attention is the product being sold.

Once you understand this, you can take back your focus. Ask yourself: *Am I in control of my scrolling, or is the app controlling me?* Awareness of this design gives you the power to choose how you spend your time online.

THE BRIGHT SIDE OF SOCIAL MEDIA

It's easy to focus on the negatives of social media—because, well, they're real. Social media can drain your time, wreck your self-esteem, and make it harder to know who and what to believe. But it's not all doom, gloom, bots, and trolls. Used with positive intentions, social media can be a space to:

- Share credible information, stories, and memes that cheer people up or make them think or laugh.

- Find others who've been through similar experiences, which can be especially comforting if you've ever felt alone, misunderstood, or like you don't fit in. For marginalized groups, these connections can be life-changing.

- Learn firsthand about other people's experiences and hear differing points of view.

- Raise awareness, challenge stereotypes, and organize around causes you care about. Social media can be a tool for action—whether it's organizing, mobilizing, or standing up for what you believe in.

Social media expresses who you are. Use it to amplify the best parts of yourself—your values, your creativity, your voice. Your actions online shape the kind of internet we all live in, so make them count for good.

TAKE THE REAL-LIFE CHALLENGE!

Social media might involve real people and real issues, but it's not the only reality—or even the best one. The world outside your phone is full of cool and fascinating people, places, and things. Spending time there can help you better understand who you are, both online and off.

So here's a challenge for you: For every hour you spend online, aim to spend another hour truly offline. Plant yourself firmly in the physical world. Hang out with friends face-to-face. Take a walk, swim, or sit and watch the moon and stars. Walk barefoot in some grass, explore your neighborhood, notice nature or the beauty on your street. Just notice the world around you.

Real life—offline life—is where the best stuff happens. Taking a break from screens is a good thing to do, really. I swear. It clears your mind. It gives you a chance to just . . . form an original thought, and appreciate the beauty all around you. It's fun to laugh for real rather than typing "LOL."

Taking a break is like closing all of the open tabs in your mind. Scrolling shows you what everyone else is doing. Taking a break gives you the chance to do things.

PAUSE BEFORE YOU POST

Take a moment to think about the last post or piece of news you shared online. Did you verify its accuracy? Did you question if it was true at all? If not, take a minute now to look it up again. Check the source, see if credible outlets are reporting the same information, and ask yourself whether your post aligns with facts.

Once that's done, think about how easy or hard it was to confirm the accuracy of your information. Did the original post come from a source you trust? If not, why did you share it? This exercise helps you see patterns in your online habits. Are you quick to share without checking? Next time, challenge yourself to pause and verify before blasting something out. This small change makes you a more informed, responsible contributor to your online world.

SPREAD THE GOOD

Since there's so much junk out there, let's focus on being part of the fun and unifying corner of the internet. For one week, challenge yourself to post or share things that don't focus on you: a favorite poem, a photo of something beautiful, someone's art, a recipe, or a story that feels good, like about a shelter dog finding a forever home. Highlight people, places, or moments that make life better, and see how it changes the vibe of your feed.

At the end of the week, look back at what you posted and how it felt. Did it shift your point of view or help you feel more cheerful? Did it lead to any new conversations or connections? Notice how sharing positive and interesting things makes an impression on others AND you. This exercise shows how social media can become a space for appreciation, creativity, and connection—when you choose to use it that way.

Save our PLANET
NO MORE HOME-WORK!
ACTIVISTS FOR ACTIVISM
Books NOT Bans

CHAPTER 8

Activism: Why Should I Care?

hen I was a junior in high school, my Ethics teacher asked if I'd give a speech in an assembly about AIDS (Acquired Immune Deficiency Syndrome). He knew I had friends living with the disease and thought I might be able to help people understand more about it. This was the late '80s, when people were scared, misinformed, and quick to judge.

To get ready, I talked with people living with AIDS. I listened to their stories of being shut out, mistreated, and constantly having to correct lies. I also did a deep dive into medical research because I wanted to be accurate.

When I stood in front of the student body, my closing message was simple: People living with AIDS deserve care, respect, and kindness. Being mean about this disease is the wrong thing to do.

Afterward, my English teacher came up to me looking emotional. She told me she'd held some harsh opinions about who got AIDS and why—but hearing my talk had shifted her thinking. It opened her mind.

That moment made a strong impression on me. It showed me that you don't have to be an expert, or have everything figured out, to speak up. I was just a regular teen, still a little self-absorbed, still learning, but I knew fairness mattered. And that day, I saw how speaking out, even in a small way, can make a difference.

Young people do make change—every single day. Take Avery Colvert, an eighth grader who started an organization called Altadena Girls to collect essentials and comforts for young women affected by wildfires in California in 2024. After her middle school burned down, Avery launched an Instagram drive to gather donations for her classmates. While food and shelter were the focus of most relief efforts, Avery recognized that small comforts like makeup, new underwear, and hair products could help teenage girls feel a sense of normality amid the sadness and devastation.

WHAT ABOUT YOU?

Anyone, anywhere, at any age can get involved, help to solve problems, and create change. What you need to get started is a cause you care about and the willingness to show up in your own way. But making a real difference starts with knowledge. Acquire that knowledge. Watch documentaries, read articles, listen to podcasts, and most importantly, talk to people who are directly affected. Be curious. Ask questions. Challenge what you think you know.

Think about what fires you up. Is it saving the bees? Fighting air pollution? Raising awareness for Crohn's disease? Once you know what moves you, learn as much as you can about it. Find organizations already doing the work and see how you can support them. Or, if nothing quite fits, consider starting something new—there are others out there who share your interests and are waiting for someone like you to lead the way.

Activism isn't always easy. There will be setbacks and roadblocks. But every deed done, every action—no matter how small—creates ripples of change. Keep going.

ROLE CALL!

Everyone has their own way to contribute, and every role matters. Getting involved takes different skills and talents. Some people thrive out front leading the way, while others prefer to work behind the scenes. Some feel pulled to handle larger organizational tasks, while others want to help out in the field. Think about what type of involvement appeals to you most. You can be a changemaker in several ways:

* **RESEARCHER:** If you have a knack for knowledge and a preference for research, your skills can provide vital information to educate people on why they should care about your cause and how they can support it. Your research can provide facts, context, and solutions to move your cause forward.
* **FACILITATOR:** If you're the person your friends turn to for advice and mediation,

your ability to bring people together can help create productive conversations—even among opponents.

- **COORDINATOR:** If you're a planner and organized, your skills can keep everyone on track toward your shared goal and ensure that people know the who, what, where, and when of your campaign.
- **ORATOR:** If public speaking interests you, use your voice to inspire and rally others into action.
- **CREATOR:** If you have an artistic touch, your work—whether it's a poem, dance, song, or painting—can move hearts and build empathy in ways numbers and facts often can't.

WHY ACTIVISM MATTERS

Activism is how you make sure your voice is part of the conversation about decisions that directly affect your life. There are people out there deciding what health care you can access, what books you can read at school, what opportunities you'll have for education and future careers—even decisions about your body. Speaking up helps these decision-makers understand what people value and need to live better, fairer lives.

But here's something essential to keep in mind: Activism needs to always consider intersectionality. This means recognizing that our identities—like race, gender, sexuality, and ability—overlap and shape how we experience the world. For example, an Indigenous girl with a disability will face challenges that are different from those of a white boy with a disability or an Indigenous boy without disabilities.

Effective activism makes sure no one is left out. A campaign for women's rights that ignores LGBTQ+ women, for instance, might accidentally exclude the very people it's trying to support. By applying intersectionality, your activism becomes more inclusive, more aware, and ultimately, more powerful.

WHY SHOULD YOU CARE?

You should care because you have the power to shape attitudes, open minds, and make life a little better for people. Whether it's speaking up, lending a hand, or supporting organizations doing the heavy lifting, you can channel your energy into something meaningful.

It's normal to feel overwhelmed by the size and complexity of the world's problems. But taking action—no matter how small—can give you a sense of purpose and help you feel like part of the solution. You don't have to go far to make good change happen; start right in your own school or neighborhood. Along the way, you'll connect with others who care as much as you do and discover more about yourself and what you believe in.

What are you waiting for? Take that first step. Contribute to a better future—you have the power, brains, and creativity to make it happen.

ACTIVISM 101

Instead of multiple opportunities for reflection here, we're going to talk about how YOU can get started making change.

1. **List three issues or causes that have caught your attention.**

   These causes are important to you for a reason—they highlight your values and what you care about most. Pay attention to patterns here. Do they involve fairness, helping people directly, protecting the environment, or breaking down barriers?

2. **Choose one of the issues from your list. Write about a personal experience with this issue or a moment when it affected you strongly.** How did that make you feel? Why do you think it matters to you now?

   Your emotional connection to this issue tells you why it resonates with you. Is it rooted in personal experience, general empathy, or something you've witnessed? This understanding can help your dedication to the cause and your direction in choosing what to do about it.

3. **Think about the change you would like to see regarding the issue you selected.** What specific changes would really help? How would these changes improve the conditions for those affected?

   Here, you identify concrete goals and outcomes. Being specific about what change looks like gives you a direction. Is the change big, like a new law, or smaller, like making someone's day-to-day life better? Recognizing this helps you focus your efforts.

4. **Consider your skills and strengths.** How can you use them to contribute to the cause you' are concerned about?

   Matching your skills with a cause makes your efforts more effective and satisfying. Are you a strong communicator, a creative thinker, or great at organizing? Your strengths are tools for contributing to change.

5. **Do some research on activists or organizations already working on this issue.** Write about one or two that inspire you. What do they do that you find admirable? How can you learn

from their actions or get involved with their efforts?

Inspiration can show you what's possible. By observing how others are making change, you can identify strategies and ideas that align with your style and goals, and then bring your unique energy to work that's already being done.

6 **Write down three steps you can take to get involved in this cause.**

Small, actionable steps make activism feel doable. Breaking your involvement into clear actions—like volunteering, writing, or fundraising—helps turn ideas into real progress.

7 **Choose one of those steps and act on it.**

CHAPTER 9

Apply the Knowledge!

hat would you tell your younger self?"

I've been asked that question in several interviews and podcasts over the years. Most people answer with a version of "It's going to be okay." But if I could sit down with my younger self, well, first, I'd have to calm her down, because meeting a time-traveling future self would definitely freak her out. Then I'd tell her the truth: "Bangs will never look good on you, but you'll keep trying them anyway. You really do move to New York City. And yes, *you're going to be okay*."

But honestly, what I think my younger self would want most is to be asked about her life. "What excites you?" "What's making you feel stuck?" "What do you care about?" She would want to know more about herself, and older me could help her dig into those questions.

Here is what I wish I had known sooner: Young adulthood is prime time to figure out who you are and who you want to become. It's a time for gathering information—exploring what you value, what excites you, and what makes you feel good about yourself. This is a time to write your own story, not follow someone else's script.

That's what I want for you: to discover what lights you up and start building a life that feels like yours. As you do that, you're going to make mistakes, lose your way, and change your mind—probably a lot. That's not failure; that's just life.

Confidence doesn't come from avoiding failure. It comes from taking risks—anywhere and everywhere—and discovering that you can thrive no matter the results. It can start on the dance floor, in a classroom, or by trying a polar plunge on New Year's Day. It builds up when you audition for a play, enter a writing contest, or speak up when it feels hard. Confidence doesn't just get a boost from the wins. It's strengthened every time you try something new, venture into the unknown, and realize you can handle whatever comes next.

APPLYING WHAT YOU'VE LEARNED

When you know yourself, it's easier to regroup, adjust, and keep going. Even so, it's still useful to have a little guidance every now and then. The tools and ideas in this book are here to help. Here are five key points in one handy-dandy little list. Keep them close, and use them when you need them.

1 Make Decisions Informed by Who YOU Are, Not Just Outside Data.

When choices feel overwhelming, return to your values. Trust your instincts—they're usually right. Develop your own definition of success and what a good life looks like. Let your choices lead you toward your version of happiness, not someone else's.

2 Cultivate Self-Compassion.

Mistakes are part of life. Treat yourself with the same kindness and patience you'd show a best friend. Learn from what happened, let it go, and keep moving forward. You deserve that.

3 Build a Support System.

Surround yourself with people who encourage and challenge you. Find friends who magnify your spirit and stick with you through the tough times. You don't need a huge circle—just people who truly get you.

4 Check in with Yourself.

Every now and then, pause and ask yourself: Am I proud of myself and my actions? Do my choices reflect the person I want to be? If the answer is no, make adjustments. Use this book as a guide when you need to realign. Revisit the questions we've discussed throughout this book and notice how your answers change over time.

5 Celebrate Accomplishments.

Progress isn't always flashy, but it deserves to be appreciated. Did you try something new? Say no to something that wasn't right for you? Finish something you started? Those moments definitely count. Celebrate them.

EQUIPPING YOURSELF FOR EVERYDAY LIFE

School teaches a lot of material—Shakespeare, continental drift, the Pythagorean theorem. But life comes with its own lessons that aren't covered in class. Here are some things to know that can help you navigate everyday situations.

How to Say "No"

"No." (It's a complete sentence.) Use it when you need to, without overexplaining or apologizing.

How to Apologize

Admit your mistake and take responsibility for who got hurt and what you did. Don't make excuses or shift the blame—just offer assurance that you'll do better from now on. Show genuine regret and take steps to make things right.

How to Stop Over-Apologizing

Apologizing for every little thing can diminish your confidence. "Sorry, can I get some water?" "Sorry, my name is actually pronounced . . ." "Sorry, I'm saying 'sorry' a lot." Give this a try: Replace "sorry" with "thank you" when appropriate. For example, instead of "Sorry for rambling," say "Thank you for listening." Save apologies for when they're truly needed.

How to Support a Friend

When someone is going through a hard time, skip vague offers like "Let me know if you need anything." Offer specific help like sharing your notes from a missed class, helping with chores, or inviting them out for iced coffee and Takis. Show you care by writing a note or simply being present. You can be supportive by sitting with someone. Just do something.

How to Ask for Help

It's normal to ask for help, so don't hesitate when you need support. First, choose someone you trust. Then, be clear about what you need help with. Share your feelings openly so they know what's going on with you emotionally, and be open to their suggestions in return. Thank them for helping, and later, let them know how the situation turned out.

How to Savor a Moment

There is a lot of advice on dealing with tough times, but we don't talk enough about how to make good moments better and longer-lasting. These moments could be something small, like when your dog snuggles up against you or receiving a text that makes you smile, or something big, like getting a part in the school play or reuniting with someone you have missed for a long time. When you notice one, don't dismiss how good the moment is. Instead, notice how you feel and let yourself enjoy that feeling fully. To take it a step further, make a conscious note of the circumstances (where you are, who you are with, what you are feeling), then write those notes down or take a picture. Think of it as documentation. Having a memory of a good moment that you can easily find helps build up faith in good things for the future.

How to Handle Embarrassment

Call it out. "Oops, I fell!" "Hey, I just called you the wrong name!" When you say it out loud, you normalize the awkwardness, and that stops negativity from taking over. Try to avoid following it up with mean self-talk like "I'm so stupid" or "I can't do anything right." Everyone gets embarrassed—no big whoop. Just apologize briefly, if an apology is necessary, and move forward with the conversation.

How to Find Humor in the Everyday

Life is full of absurdity, like waving at someone who was definitely waving at the person behind you, or realizing halfway through the day that your shirt has been on inside out. You can either cringe or laugh. Go with laughter. Life is weird, you're weird, and we're all better for it.

How to Volunteer at an Animal Shelter

(I just think everyone should know how to do this.) Volunteering at a shelter is an awesome thing you can do for both you and the dogs. Find your local shelter and ask about their volunteer policies, age requirements, and how to register. Once you're set up, you can take a dog for a walk. Even a short walk gives dogs exercise, fresh air, and breaks from their kennels. It's easy and brightens the dog's day, and it will make your day better, too.

WHAT COMES NEXT? GO LIVE YOUR LIFE

Your "real life" isn't waiting for you at the next milestone: college, your own apartment, the dream job, the epic romance. It's happening right now, in small, surprising moments: the laugh-out-loud conversation with your best friend, the song you sing along with, the detour that turns into an adventure. Notice these moments, and let them teach you something about yourself.

Getting to know yourself happens by living—by saying yes to experiences, following your curiosity, and noticing what makes you feel most alive. Sleep under the stars. Walk a different route. Look up at the clouds. Be curious about people whose lives are nothing like yours. Take risks, keep playing, and keep asking questions. And—this is important—don't ditch what you love just because someone else thinks it's uncool. Liking what you like is cool.

You don't have to know exactly where you're headed or what's next. Plans will change. You will change. That's okay. Life is unpredictable, and the in-between moments, the messy moments, and the unplanned moments are much of what make up a life.

ONE LAST THING

The world doesn't need a perfect version of you. It just needs you. Your quirks, your ideas, your unique self.

The life you want is built one choice, one experience, and one step at a time. So take your time. Trust yourself. And remember: you're doing great. I'm rooting for you every step of the way.

P. S. BE YOURSELF.

ACKNOWLEDGMENTS

I loved writing this book and I was able to do it because of all the time I've spent with girls through the years. Thank you to every girl who has welcomed me into their life and shared their stories with me—you are the heart of this book. A special extra-big thank-you to the lovely and amazing Riley Hochwald.

To my mother, Liz Walker, whose extraordinary humor and sharp intelligence have been my guiding light since I was born. Thank you for your love and support, and for making us a family of critical thinkers who love each other.

To my father, Jeffrey Walker, whose collaboration and invaluable input have been the foundation of this book. Your ethical guidance and thoughtful contributions have improved every page. You're the secret weapon behind this book and I couldn't have done it without you.

Thank you to my favorite people: my brother, Christopher Walker, and my sister, Megan Miles. Your willingness to still take my calls, no matter how many times I needed your help, means more to me than words can express. Your wise counsel, gentle teasing, and unusable jokes have kept me going. I love y'all so much!

Thank you to the wonderful people at Workman Publishing. Stacy Lellos gave encouraging feedback that made me want to write my heart out. Karen Smith advocated for this book in its early stages and wisely advised me to delete references so old they should be under glass in the Smithsonian.

A very special thank-you to my editor, Cheryl Klein, for being the kind of wise collaborator writers dream of working with. Your thoughtful questions and intelligent contributions absolutely turned this book into something of which to be proud. Thank you for working so hard and putting in extra time to elevate this book to a new level. I'm truly fortunate to have your expertise.

I owe a heartfelt thanks to my literary agents at WME: Sabrina Taitz, who believed this book was worth championing, and Sian-Ashleigh Edwards, who worked diligently to help shape the idea from the beginning and along the way helped shape my understanding of the publishing world. What a great team!

I'm fortunate to have smart, generous, and funny friends willing to read early drafts and offer wisdom and advice. Thank you to Wendi Aarons, Anne Hebert, Laura Mayes, Shellie McMahon, Kathy Valentine, and Jennifer Treat.

For unwavering moral support even from far away: Thank you to Maya Rudolph, Mark Sullivan, Sean Hayes, Amy Miles, and Emily Spivey. Thank you for being my friends through time and distance.

For teaching me to never dilute the truth no matter the age of the viewer or reader, thank you to Linda Ellerbee and Mark Lyons. I couldn't have asked for better mentors. And I promise to never use "task" as a verb.

For boosting my confidence as I wrote, thank you to Kit and Marti Walsh, Jon and Keith Meacham, Jen Stone, Maggie Chieffo, Heather Howard, Michelle Lewis, Brumby Boylston, Stacie Walker, Jack Walker, Alex Goldsmith, Kelly Black, Amy Arrowsmith, Charley Crichton, Maryetta Anschutz, Joel Mozersky, Leila Miles, Walker Miles, and Will Miles.

Thank you to Word Of Mouth Provisions for the comforting hospitality.

Thank you to everyone at the Ann Richards School for Young Women Leaders, especially Christena Rutz, who guided me to mentor students and supported Smart Girls from the very beginning.

Deepest gratitude to Amy Poehler, creator of the very best itineraries and a world-champ good listener. When you make your chicken curry for me, I feel safe and loved. Thank you for twenty-five years of outstanding service in the field of friendship.

And to Tom, thank you for our wonderful life.

Meredith Walker began her career in journalism at the groundbreaking Nickelodeon series *Nick News*. She worked her way up from production assistant to segment producer, traveling the country to interview kids, experts, politicians, and artists for news stories. She later moved to *Saturday Night Live*, where she ran the talent department, before she and Amy Poehler cofounded Smart Girls, an online community that encourages young women to celebrate who they are and who they are becoming.

Through programs, workshops, and day camps, Meredith has helped girls try new things and discover more about themselves. That work has taken her from classrooms and regional programs to the White House, the United Nations, and communities around the world. She now lives in Austin, Texas, with her longtime love, Tom, and their dogs Banjo and Farris.

Nina Cosford has illustrated more than twenty books. She lives in the United Kingdom. Find her online at ninacosford.com.